Things to Know About Starting or Investing in a Hair Salon

Disclaimer:

The information contained in this book is provided for general informational purposes only. While every effort has been made to ensure that the information is accurate and up-to-date, The Author makes no representations or warranties of any kind, express or implied, about the completeness, accuracy, reliability, suitability, or availability with respect to the information, products, services, or related graphics contained in the book for any purpose.

The Author disclaims any liability for any loss or damage, including without limitation, indirect or consequential loss or damage, or any loss or damage whatsoever arising from loss of data or profits arising out of, or in connection with, the use of this book.

Readers are solely responsible for determining the appropriateness of the information contained in this book for their specific purposes and should seek professional advice before acting upon any information contained herein. The Author shall not be liable for any damages of any kind arising from the use of this book or the information contained herein.

Table of Contents

Introduction

Starting or investing in a hair salon is an exciting and challenging undertaking. Whether you are a seasoned business owner or a first-time entrepreneur, there are numerous terms and concepts to know in order to make informed decisions and ultimately achieve success in this industry. From leasing a space to purchasing equipment, hiring employees to creating a marketing plan, there is a lot to consider when starting or investing in a hair salon.

This glossary-type book contains a comprehensive list of terms and definitions related to starting or investing in a hair salon. It serves as a resource for anyone looking to enter or expand into this field, providing clarity and understanding on topics such as salon management, finances, marketing, and more. Whether you are looking to start your own salon or invest in an existing one, this book will provide you with the knowledge and understanding needed to make informed decisions and excel in the hair salon industry.

Accounting

The systematic recording, reporting, and analysis of financial transactions. Understanding basic accounting principles can help hair salon owners keep track of cash flow, manage expenses, and make informed business decisions.

Accreditation

The process of obtaining recognition or certification from a professional organization or institution for meeting certain standards. A hair salon that has been accredited can provide customers with a sense of trust and credibility.

Advertising

The act of promoting a business using various techniques such as paid ads, online marketing or social media campaigns. Effective advertising can be a key strategy in attracting and retaining customers for your hair salon.

Amenities

Additional features or services that a hair salon may offer to enhance the customer experience, such as refreshments, high-end products, or comfortable seating. Offering attractive amenities can help differentiate your hair salon from competitors.

Analysis

The process of examining data and information to identify patterns and trends that can inform decision-making. Conducting regular analysis of various aspects of a hair salon, such as customer preferences or inventory levels, can help improve business performance.

Apprenticeship

A program that involves learning a trade or craft by working under the supervision of a skilled professional. An apprenticeship in the hair salon industry can provide hands-on experience and practical knowledge.

Architecture

The design and layout of a hair salon, including the structural components, aesthetics, and function. Choosing the right architecture and design is crucial to creating a comfortable and inviting space for customers.

Assets

Things to help generate income such as equipment, furniture, and inventory that are owned rather than leased. Knowing how to value and acquire the right assets for a hair salon can help ensure that it is profitable and serves its intended purpose.

Attitude

A positive and proactive mindset that can help hair salon owners overcome challenges and adapt to changing circumstances. Cultivating a can-do attitude can help foster a supportive and creative environment that attracts and retains customers.

Autonomy

The ability to make independent decisions and operate a hair salon without excessive oversight or interference. Maintaining autonomy can provide salon owners with greater control over business operations and decision-making.

Basic Equipment

The essential tools and equipment needed to run a hair salon. This includes items such as styling chairs, washbasins, hair dryers, combs and brushes, and styling products. Investing in quality equipment is important for providing a comfortable and professional environment for clients and for ensuring the safety of stylists.

Bookkeeping

The practice of recording and tracking all financial transactions related to a hair salon. This includes income from services and product sales, as well as expenses such as rent, utilities, and supplies. Accurate bookkeeping is crucial for managing cash flow, filing taxes, and making informed business decisions.

Booth Renting

An arrangement in which hair stylists and other salon professionals rent a booth or chair in a salon to provide their services. This allows them to work independently without the overhead costs of owning their own salon. Salon owners benefit by collecting rent from multiple professionals and by having a diverse range of services available to their clients.

Brand Ambassadors

Individuals who promote and represent a hair salon's brand and services to their networks and followers. This may include social media influencers, satisfied customers, and other local advocates. Brand ambassadors can help expand the salon's reach and build a loyal customer base.

Branding

The process of creating a distinct and recognizable identity for a hair salon. This includes choosing a name, color scheme, logo, and other branding elements that convey the salon's style and philosophy. A strong brand can help attract and retain customers, and differentiate the salon from its competitors.

Break-Even Point

The point at which a hair salon's total revenue equals its total expenses. This is an important metric for understanding the financial health of the business and for planning future investments. It can also help determine pricing strategies and marketing efforts.

Budgeting

The process of creating and managing a plan for allocating financial resources within a hair salon. This includes setting goals and priorities, estimating income and expenses, and monitoring actual spending. Effective budgeting is critical for ensuring the salon has the resources it needs to succeed and for avoiding financial challenges.

Business Insurance

A type of insurance that protects a hair salon from financial loss due to property damage, liability claims, and other unforeseen events. This may include coverage for theft, fire, natural disasters, and accidents that occur on the salon premises. It is important to carefully evaluate and select the right insurance policies to mitigate risks and protect the business.

Business License

A document that allows a hair salon to legally operate in a specific area. The requirements for obtaining a business license vary by location, but typically include registering with the state or local government, paying fees, and meeting certain health and safety standards.

Business Plan

A detailed document that outlines the goals, strategies, and financial projections for a hair salon. A well-written business plan is essential for securing funding and for laying out a clear path for success. It should address topics such as the salon's services, target market, competitive landscape, staffing needs, and revenue streams.

Cash flow

Refers to the amount of money coming in and out of your salon's accounts. A consistent cash flow is necessary to cover salon expenses such as rent, utilities, and staff payments. Maintaining a good cash flow requires careful financial planning and effective management of salon finances, including tracking expenses and setting aside profits for future investments.

Certifications

Refers to the industry-recognized qualifications that hairstylists can earn to showcase their skill and knowledge. Certifications prove that hairstylists have the necessary credentials to perform specific services and satisfy clients' needs, increasing the salon's credibility. Some popular certifications include cosmetology licenses, hair extensions certifications, and balayage certifications.

Clientele

Refers to the customers who frequent the hair salon. It is essential to understand the target market to attract the right clientele to your salon. A clear understanding of your ideal client's needs, preferences, and spending habits will help you tailor your services and pricing accordingly. It is also essential to communicate with them effectively to build lasting relationships.

Compensation

Refers to the salaries and wages paid to employees of the hair salon. Pay scales for hairstylists typically vary by their experience, skillset, and certifications. Setting fair and competitive compensation packages will help attract and retain quality staff members, improving your salon's performance.

Competition

Refers to the other hair salons in your area catering to the same clientele. Conducting market research to understand the competition's services, pricing, and marketing strategy is vital to establishing a distinctive position in the market. It will help you create unique offerings, pricing, and promotions that set you apart from competitors.

Compliance

Refers to adhering to rules, regulations, and legal requirements in the operation of the salon. Compliance includes following local, state, and federal laws and regulations governing the salon industry. Ensuring compliance with regulations such as licensing requirements, building codes, and health and safety standards will help avoid legal consequences and enhance the salon's reputation.

Contracts

Refers to the legal agreements binding between the hair salon and its employees, suppliers, or business partners. Contracts outline the obligations, rights, and responsibilities of each party, establishing clarity, and protection in case of any legal disputes. Hiring a qualified attorney to draft contracts ensures efficient and fair agreements, safeguarding the salon's interests.

Cost of goods sold

Refers to the expenses incurred in delivering a service or product, including inventory or product purchases, packaging, and shipping. Understanding and managing the cost of goods sold is essential to an efficient operational model, costing pricing, and profitability. Overhead, labor, and expenses must be factored in to ensure the hair salon is profitable.

Credibility

Refers to your salon's reputation and standing in the community. Creating a credible brand image requires providing high-quality services, excellent customer service, and investing in marketing efforts. Building trust with your customers and having positive reviews online and through word-of-mouth marketing can significantly impact your salon's success.

Customer service

Refers to how your salon treats its customers. Superior customer service is critical to enhancing customer satisfaction and loyalty, resulting in new and loyal customers. Providing quality services, being responsive to customer feedback, and providing a welcoming atmosphere will create an excellent customer experience and help build a positive reputation for your salon.

Daily Operations

Refers to the tasks and activities that need to be performed on a daily basis to keep your salon running smoothly. This includes staffing, scheduling, inventory management, marketing, and more. Planning and organizing your daily operations is essential for the success of your salon.

Décor

Refers to the overall style and aesthetic of your salon. Creating a welcoming and visually appealing salon atmosphere is important in attracting and retaining customers. Choose a décor style that aligns with your branding and target audience.

Demand

Refers to the desire of customers for a particular product or service. Before investing in a hair salon, it's important to research and analyze the demand for hair services in your area. This can help you determine the potential success and profitability of your salon.

Demographics

Refers to the population of a particular area and their characteristics such as age, gender, income, and education level. Knowing the demographics of your location can help you tailor your services and marketing strategies to attract potential customers.

Distributors

Refers to companies that supply hair products and tools to salons. It's important to choose reliable and quality distributors to ensure you are providing your customers with the best products available.

E-commerce

The buying and selling of goods and services online. Integrating e-commerce into your hair salon website can increase revenue and streamline the booking process for clients. Consider selling hair products or gift cards online, and implementing online booking and payment options.

Education

Continuing education for yourself and your employees is essential to remain up-to-date on industry developments and best practices. Attend hair shows and workshops, and consider offering training sessions or classes for your employees to enhance their skills.

Employee Contracts

Formal agreements between an employer and employees outlining the terms of employment, including salary, benefits, and expectations. Creating clear and detailed contracts protects both the employer and employees, preventing misunderstandings and legal issues later on. Consult with a lawyer to ensure that your contracts are legal and enforceable.

End-of-Day Procedures

The tasks and routines that should be completed by salon employees before closing for the day, such as cleaning, restocking supplies, and closing out cash drawers. Establishing clear end-of-day procedures ensures that your salon remains organized and efficient.

Engagement

The level of interaction and communication between a salon and its clients. Engaging with clients through social media, email marketing, and loyalty programs can create a loyal and satisfied customer base. Consider offering promotions or hosting events to encourage client engagement and build relationships.

Entrepreneur

A person who starts and runs a business. Starting a hair salon requires an entrepreneurial spirit and willingness to take risks. Learn from other successful entrepreneurs, and seek out mentorship and guidance when necessary.

Equipment

The tools and devices used in a hair salon, such as scissors, blow dryers, and styling chairs. Having high-quality equipment is essential for creating a professional and efficient salon environment. Before investing in equipment, research different brands and read reviews to ensure that you are making the best purchase for your salon's needs and budget.

Esthetic

The overall look and feel of a hair salon, including the decor, lighting, and ambiance. Establishing a cohesive aesthetic can create a memorable and inviting experience for clients. Consider hiring a professional interior designer to create a unique and attractive space.

Estimation

Calculating the costs and potential profits of a new salon. Conduct market research and create a detailed business plan to estimate your salon's potential revenue and expenses. Ensure that your estimates are realistic and based on data, rather than assumptions.

Expenses

The costs associated with running a hair salon, including rent, utilities, supplies, and employee salaries. It's crucial to have a detailed understanding of your expenses to create a realistic budget and ensure that your salon remains profitable.

Financial Statement

A financial statement is a summary report of the financial transactions that occur in a business. It includes an income statement, balance sheet, and cash flow statement. Financial statements help you understand the financial health of your salon, track expenses, and improve decision-making based on financial data.

Financing

You may need financing to start or expand your hair salon, and there are several options available. You can apply for a small business loan, use a credit card, gain investors, or use personal funds. It is essential to research and compare interest rates, repayment plans, and terms to find the best option for your business.

Finishing Touches

Finishing touches include the extras that make your salon stand out to clients, such as quality product lines, decorative design elements, and luxurious amenities like refreshments and comfortable seating. These touches can help create a unique experience that separates your salon from competitors and keeps customers coming back.

Fixed Costs

Fixed costs are the overhead expenses that don't fluctuate with the number of clients you have, such as rent, insurance, and utilities. These costs can add up quickly and will impact your monthly budget, so you must plan accordingly.

Floor Plan

The floor plan of your salon determines the flow of traffic and the functionality of your space. Before opening, design your floor plan to consider customer flow, workspace, storage, restrooms, and break areas. Take advantage of natural light, ensure adequate ventilation, and make sure the layout supports ADA accessibility and safety codes.

Follow-Up

Follow-up is a vital aspect of any beauty business. It involves reaching out to clients through phone calls, texts, or emails to thank them for their patronage or update them on new services or products. Consistent follow-up builds customer loyalty and increases the likelihood of repeat business.

Forecasting

Forecasting is the process of predicting customer demand, revenue, and expenses for your hair salon. It helps your business set strategic goals, create focused marketing strategies, and make informed decisions related to growth and expansion.

Franchise

A franchise is a business model where a salon owner can use the trademark, business model, and support of an established hair salon in exchange for a fee. This would allow you to have access to well-known brand name recognition and immediate customer base, but it also means you may have to follow strict guidelines and pay ongoing royalties or fees to the franchisor.

Freelance Stylists

Freelance stylists are independent contractors who work inside salon spaces. They provide their own tools, manage their own schedules, and may bring their clientele to your salon. Hiring freelance stylists provides flexibility with staffing, but it also requires you to balance schedules, maintain relationships with stylists, and manage conflicts between stylists.

Furniture

The furniture in your salon is an essential part of your business as it impacts the overall aesthetic and comfort of your customers. Styling chairs, shampoo bowls, waiting area chairs, and storage units are all pieces you must consider when creating your salon layout. Your furniture should be comfortable and functional, but it should also align with your salon's brand image and theme.

Goodwill

The value of the salon's reputation, client base, and brand image in the community. Goodwill is not a tangible asset, but it can have a significant impact on the value of the salon and the success of the business. Potential salon owners should consider the existing goodwill when determining whether to invest in or start a salon.

Government Regulations

Laws and regulations set forth by local, state, and federal governments that salons must comply with to operate legally. Regulations can include licensing requirements, safety regulations, and sanitation standards.

Gross Profit

The amount of money left after the cost of goods sold and all other expenses have been deducted from the total revenue generated by the salon. Calculating gross profit is essential for business owners to understand how much money is being made and the overall profitability of the salon.

Group Bookings

Reservations made for multiple people at the same time, such as bridal parties, corporate events, or group haircuts. Group bookings can be a significant source of revenue for salons but require advanced planning and coordination.

Growth Potential

The ability of a salon to expand and increase its revenue and profitability over time. Factors such as the salon's location, client base, and services offered can all impact its growth potential.

Growth Strategy

A plan for expanding and growing the salon's business, which may include adding new services, expanding to multiple locations, or increasing marketing efforts. A well-developed growth strategy is essential for the long-term success of the salon.

Guarantees

Promises made by the salon to clients, such as a guarantee that the client will be satisfied with the service. Guarantees can help build trust and confidence with customers, but they must be realistic and achievable to avoid disappointing clients.

Guest Cancellation policy

The guidelines that the salon has in place for clients who cancel appointments. These policies often dictate whether clients will be charged for missed appointments or required to give notice of cancellation in advance. An effective cancellation policy can help reduce no-shows and increase revenue for the salon.

Guest Experience

The overall experience that a client has when visiting the salon, including the quality of services, customer service, and the salon environment. A positive guest experience can lead to repeat business and referrals.

Guest Retention

The ability of the salon to retain customers and keep them coming back for repeat business. High guest retention rates are crucial for the long-term success of a salon and can be achieved through excellent customer service, quality services, and a welcoming atmosphere.

Hair Care Products

Specialized products designed for hair maintenance and styling including shampoo, conditioner, mousse, hair spray, and hair coloring products. A hair salon must carry high-quality and reliable hair care products to help maintain healthy hair and meet the diverse needs of its clients.

Hair Salon Business Plan

A strategic plan that outlines the objectives, goals and projections for a hair salon. A good business plan helps entrepreneurs determine the feasibility of their salon and set goals for growth, expansion, and profitability.

Hair Salon Finances

The management of a salon's financial resources, including budgeting, expenses, and revenues. Proper financial management is essential to the survival and growth of a hair salon business.

Hair Salon Marketing

A marketing strategy used to promote hair salon services to potential customers. This can include advertising online or in local publications, attending community events, and offering discounts or promotions to new or returning customers. Effective marketing is key to attracting new clients and increasing visibility within the community.

Hair Salon Owner

A person who owns and manages a hair salon. A hair salon owner handles everything from managing stylists to ensuring customer satisfaction. They must be knowledgeable about the industry, have excellent communication and organizational skills and be able to market and advertise their salon effectively. Hair salon owners also need to build good relationships with their clients and provide quality service to maintain the reputation of their salon.

Hair Styling Techniques

Methods and techniques used by stylists to achieve various hairstyles, including cuts, colors, perms, and extensions. Good training and experience with a variety of hair styling techniques can help increase the quality of service provided by a hair salon and its reputation.

Hair Styling Tools

Equipment used by stylists to style hair. Examples include scissors, combs, hairdryers, curling irons, and straighteners. It's important to invest in high-quality tools that last longer and perform better for the benefit of clients and the salon's reputation.

Hours of Operation

The time a hair salon operates, including opening hours and closing hours. Hours of operation can vary depending on the location, the target audience, and the services offered. Hair salon owners must consider the hours of operation that are most convenient for their local demographic and align with their business goals.

Human Resource Management

The process of hiring and managing employees. This includes conducting interviews, hiring, training, and firing employees. Good human resource management practices lead to happier and more productive employees, which in turn can help improve the reputation of the salon.

Hygiene

The practice of maintaining clean and safe working conditions. This includes sterilization of equipment and tools, the use of clean towels and gowns for each customer, and maintaining a clean workspace. Good hygiene is important in a hair salon because it provides a safe and healthy environment for clients and employees.

Income Forecasting

The process of estimating future income of a hair salon. This includes analyzing historical data, market trends, marketing strategies, and expenses. Income forecasting helps to identify potential revenue streams, plan for seasonal changes, and understand the cash flow of the business.

Industry Regulations

The guidelines and regulations that govern the hair salon industry. This includes compliance with state and federal regulations, health and safety requirements, licensing, and certification. It's important to stay up-to-date with the latest regulations to avoid penalties, lawsuits, and reputational damage.

Industry Trends

The evolving trends, practices, and styles within the hair salon industry. This includes new technologies, techniques, products, and services, as well as changes in consumer preferences. Being aware of industry trends helps to stay competitive, offer innovative services, and meet the changing demands of the market.

Infrastructure

The physical and technological elements of a hair salon that support the daily operations of the business. This includes the layout of the space, lighting, electrical, plumbing, phone and internet systems, and software for scheduling, booking appointments, and managing finances. A well-planned infrastructure ensures the efficiency, productivity, and profitability of the business.

Initial Investment

The initial amount of money needed to start a hair salon. This includes the cost of leasing or buying a space, purchasing equipment and supplies, hiring staff, and marketing the business. An accurate estimate of the initial investment can help to secure funding and ensure the financial stability of the salon.

Insurance Coverage

The coverage that a hair salon needs to protect the business from risks and liability. This includes general liability insurance, professional liability insurance or malpractice insurance, worker's compensation insurance, and property insurance. Proper insurance coverage can help to mitigate financial loss in case of accidents, injuries, and damages.

Interior Design

The process of designing the interior of a hair salon to attract and retain customers. This includes selecting a color scheme, choosing furniture and fixtures, and creating an ambiance that reflects the image of the salon. Interior design plays a critical role in attracting a specific target market, making the space visually appealing, and creating a comfortable environment for the clients and staff.

Internal Controls

The systems and procedures that ensure the accuracy and reliability of financial and operational data within a hair salon. This includes recordkeeping, financial reporting, cash handling, and security measures. Proper internal controls reduce the risk of errors, fraud, and theft, and improve transparency and accountability.

Inventory Management

The process of keeping track of all the products, supplies and materials needed to run a successful hair salon. This includes stock levels, ordering, and tracking of the salon's inventory. Proper inventory management ensures that you never run out of supplies, identify fast-moving items, avoid overstocking, and reduce the risk of theft or damage.

Investor Relations

The way in which a hair salon communicates with its investors and stakeholders. This includes investor presentations, annual reports, financial statements, and regular updates on the company's performance. Effective investor relations can help to build trust, confidence, and support for the business, and attract new investors and partners.

Jargon

The specialized language used in the hair salon industry, such as terms for different types of haircuts or coloring techniques. New employees will need to learn this language to communicate effectively with clients and other team members.

Job Duties

The specific tasks that each employee is responsible for in the hair salon, such as cutting hair, coloring, and styling. It's essential to clarify job duties upfront to eliminate confusion and ensure everyone knows their responsibilities.

Job Satisfaction

Ensuring that employees enjoy their work and find it fulfilling is essential for employee retention and the salon's overall success. Providing training opportunities, clear expectations, and a positive work environment can help increase job satisfaction among salon employees.

Job Shadowing

A process where aspiring salon employees observe and learn from experienced professionals in the salon. It can help new employees learn the salon's culture and workflows, and it's a great way to provide on-the-job training.

Join Professional Associations

Joining professional associations can provide networking opportunities, access to industry events and training, and other valuable resources for salon owners and managers.

Journaling

Keeping a journal can help salon owners and managers keep track of expenses, record insights on industry trends and customer preferences, and reflect on their successes and challenges.

Judgement

The ability to make sound decisions and use good judgement is essential for success in the hair salon industry. Owners and managers need to make decisions based on data and sound reasoning to ensure the salon's profitability and growth.

Juice Bar

Many hair salons now include juice bars as part of their offerings, providing healthy drinks to clients while they get their hair done. A juice bar can boost a salon's revenue and provide a unique experience for clients.

Just-in-time inventory

The practice of ordering and receiving only the materials and supplies needed for the salon's daily operations, rather than stockpiling excess inventory. This approach can help save money and reduce waste in the salon's budget.

Juxtaposition

The arrangement of different elements, such as colors or textures, to create contrast and interest in the salon's decor. A salon's decor should appeal to its target audience and represent the salon's brand and personality.

Karma

In the hair salon business, karma refers to the positive reputation and goodwill that a salon has built up over time. Having a strong reputation for quality service, fair pricing, and a welcoming atmosphere can attract repeat customers and help the salon to grow.

Keeping Records

Keeping accurate records is essential for any salon that wants to succeed. This can include detailed financial records, employee schedules, client information, and more. By keeping organized and detailed records, salon owners can make informed decisions about how to grow their business.

Kettle

A kettle is a small appliance that is used in salons to heat water for tea or coffee. While a kettle may seem like a minor item, it can make a big difference in creating a welcoming atmosphere for clients and staff.

Key Performance Indicators (KPIs)

Metrics that are used to track the performance of a hair salon, such as average ticket value, customer retention rate, and employee productivity. KPIs help salon owners to identify areas where they need to improve and make data-driven decisions about how to grow their business.

Key Personnel

Personnel are the people who work in a hair salon, and key personnel refers to those individuals who are instrumental in running the business. This can include stylists, receptionists, managers, and marketing staff.

Kickback

A kickback is a payment or other incentive that is given to someone as a reward for bringing in new customers or sales. While kickbacks can be an effective marketing tool, they can also be illegal in some jurisdictions and can damage the reputation of a salon if not done ethically.

Kiosk

A small, standalone station that is used for selling products or services in a hair salon. Kiosks can be used to sell hair care products or to offer quick services like blowouts or touch-ups.

Kit

A collection of tools and products that are essential for running a hair salon. This can include items like scissors, blow dryers, and hair dye. Investing in a high-quality kit is crucial for ensuring that your salon provides top-notch service and stays competitive in the industry.

Knowledge

One of the most important assets for anyone starting or investing in a hair salon is knowledge. This involves understanding the latest trends in hair styling and color, tips for managing staff and client relationships, and being up-to-date on the latest industry news.

KPI Dashboard

A KPI dashboard is a digital tool that is used to track and analyze key performance indicators in real-time. Using a KPI dashboard can make it easier for salon owners to spot trends, identify potential problems, and make data-driven decisions about their business.

Labor Laws

Refers to the various regulations set by the government to ensure fair working environment. It is important to be well-versed in labor laws before starting or investing in a hair salon to avoid any legal issues in the future. It includes minimum wage, overtime, break time, employment contracts, discrimination, and health and safety regulations.

Layout

The arrangement of space in the hair salon. It is important to have a functional and efficient layout to ensure smooth operations and a comfortable experience for clients. This includes the placement of chairs, stations, sinks, mirrors, storage, and waiting area, as well as the flow of traffic and accessibility for clients with special needs.

Lease Agreement

A legal contract between the landlord and the tenant, outlining the terms and conditions of renting the property. Before starting or investing in a hair salon, it is important to carefully review and negotiate lease agreements to ensure favorable terms, such as rent amount, lease length, renewability, and maintenance responsibilities.

Liability Insurance

Insurance that covers damages and legal costs in case of accidents or injuries in the hair salon. It is important to have liability insurance before starting or investing in a hair salon to protect the business and its assets in case of unforeseen incidents or lawsuits.

Licensing

The process of obtaining the necessary permits and certifications from the government or relevant agencies to legally operate a hair salon. It includes business licenses, cosmetology licenses, and permits for health and safety regulations. It is important to be familiar with the licensing requirements in the specific location before starting or investing in a hair salon.

Location

The geographical area where the hair salon is situated. It is important to carefully choose a location that is easily accessible, visible, and near the target market. It is also important to consider factors such as rent, competition, public transport, and parking availability when deciding on the location.

Logo

A visual representation of the hair salon brand that is used in marketing and advertising materials. It is important to design a unique and memorable logo that represents the salon's values and services. A well-designed logo can help attract and retain customers, and build brand awareness and loyalty.

Loyalty Program

A marketing strategy that rewards loyal customers with discounts, promotions, or exclusive services. It is important to establish a loyalty program to incentivize clients to return and refer others to the hair salon. This can help increase sales and build customer loyalty and satisfaction.

Maintenance and upkeep

Maintenance and upkeep refer to the ongoing process of keeping the salon clean, organized, and well-maintained. This includes tasks such as cleaning the salon regularly, updating equipment, and keeping tabs on inventory levels.

Management software

Management software refers to specialized digital tools that can help manage different aspects of a hair salon business. Management software is crucial for tasks such as appointment scheduling, employee management, inventory management, payroll, and accounting.

Management team

The management team includes managers and other key personnel who oversee the day-to-day operations of the hair salon. Ensuring that you have a strong and experienced management team in place is key to the success of any salon.

Market analysis

Market analysis refers to the process of assessing the local market, competitors, and potential customers of a hair salon. A thorough market analysis helps you identify existing gaps in services, understand the spending habits of potential customers, and create tailored marketing plans.

Marketing strategy

A marketing strategy encompasses all the tactics, techniques, and tools used to promote a hair salon business. A successful marketing strategy should consider factors such as target market, competition, pricing, and advertising methods.

Menu of Services

A menu of services is an outline of all available services that a hair salon provides. It is important to have a clear menu of services that accurately represents the salon's offerings and pricing.

Merchandising

Merchandising refers to the process of displaying and promoting retail products sold in the salon. Effective merchandising strategies help generate additional revenue and create a more attractive environment for customers.

Microblading

Microblading is a semi-permanent cosmetic technique used to enhance eyebrow shape and fullness. As a popular service in many hair salons, it is important to understand the technique and ensure that the salon has the right equipment and trained staff.

Mobile salon

A mobile salon is a unique business model that involves delivering salon services to clients at their homes or workplaces. Operating a mobile salon comes with its own unique challenges, such as ensuring that equipment is well-maintained and that appropriate transportation is available.

Modern design

Modern design refers to the aesthetic and layout of a hair salon. With the industry constantly evolving, it is important that a hair salon stays up-to-date with modern design trends to help create a welcoming atmosphere and attract customers.

Natural hair care

A hair care method that involves using all-natural and organic products to promote healthy hair growth without the use of chemicals. Natural hair care may include using essential oils, plant-based ingredients, and avoiding heat styling tools to maintain the hair's natural state. Offering natural hair care services can attract customers interested in holistic health and wellness.

Net profit

The amount of revenue left after all expenses are paid, including rent, utilities, supplies, and payroll. Accurately calculating net profit is crucial for determining the financial health of a hair salon and making informed business decisions.

Networking

Building relationships with other salon owners, industry professionals, and community members to promote a hair salon and collaboration. Networking can provide opportunities for new business, referrals, and staying up-to-date on industry trends and best practices.

New hire onboarding

The process of introducing and training new employees on salon policies, procedures, and expectations. Proper onboarding can help new hires feel welcome, understand their roles, and provide consistent customer service.

Niche

A targeted market or specialized service offered within the broader hair salon industry to differentiate a business from competitors. A niche may include the use of organic and eco-friendly products, catering to a specific demographic, or specializing in a particular hair service.

Non-compete agreement

A legally binding document that prohibits former employees or owners from working for competing businesses within a specific geographic area for a set period after leaving the salon. A non-compete agreement can protect a salon's trade secrets, client list, and prevent competitors from poaching employees.

Non-toxic hair dyes

Hair color that is free from harmful ingredients such as ammonia, resorcinol, and parabens. Non-toxic hair dyes are becoming increasingly popular among clients who are mindful of their health and the environment, and salons may choose to offer these options to meet customer demand.

No-poo

A hair care method that involves washing hair without traditional shampoos containing harsh chemicals like sulfates. No-poo products may contain gentler ingredients like apple cider vinegar, baking soda, or co-washes that can be beneficial for clients with specific hair needs.

No-shows

Clients who fail to show up for their scheduled hair appointments, resulting in lost revenue and wasted appointment time. A no-show policy can be implemented to minimize the impact of missed appointments, including requiring prepayment or charging a fee for no-shows.

Nosocomial infections

Infections that originate in hospitals or other healthcare settings that can be transmitted to clients during hair services. Proper sanitation protocols can prevent the spread of nosocomial infections, including washing hands, sanitizing surfaces and tools, and using disposable items where possible.

Offerings

A hair salon's offerings include the services and products it provides to customers. These may include haircuts, coloring, styling, and products such as shampoos and conditioners. It's important to choose offerings carefully based on the target market, competition, and staffing capabilities.

Online Presence

A hair salon's online presence includes its website, social media accounts, and online reviews. This is a crucial element in marketing and building a brand. Having an appealing website with easy-to-use booking features, a social media strategy, and positive reviews can attract new customers and retain existing ones.

Opening a Hair Salon

Before opening a hair salon, it's important to develop a business plan, secure funding, find a location, acquire necessary licenses and permits, purchase essential equipment and supplies, and hire skilled employees. A successful opening requires careful planning, market research, and a thorough understanding of the hair salon industry.

Operating Costs

Operating costs are the ongoing expenses required to keep the hair salon running. This includes rent, utilities, payroll, supplies, and marketing expenses. Managing operating costs is crucial to maintaining a healthy profit margin and ensuring the long-term success of the business.

Operations

Refers to the day-to-day running of the hair salon. This includes scheduling appointments, managing employees, handling payments, ordering supplies, and ensuring customer satisfaction. Operations are crucial in maintaining a successful business and require careful planning and organization.

Organization

A well-organized hair salon is essential for efficiency and productivity. This includes maintaining a clean and tidy workspace, keeping track of appointments, inventory, and finances, and having clear communication channels with employees and customers.

Outsourcing

Outsourcing refers to hiring outside professionals or companies to provide specific services such as accounting, marketing, or IT. Outsourcing can save money and increase efficiency, but it's important to carefully vet and communicate with these third-party providers to ensure quality work and protect the salon's reputation.

Overhead

The expenses required to keep the hair salon running that are not directly related to producing income. This includes rent, utilities, insurance, and taxes. It's important to calculate overhead costs accurately to determine the pricing strategy, break-even point, and profit margins for the hair salon.

Owner's Role

The owner's role includes overseeing the operations of the hair salon, managing finances, developing a business strategy, and leading the team. The owner must have a clear vision of the business's goals and communicate effectively with employees, customers, and stakeholders.

Ownership Structure

The ownership structure of a hair salon determines how the business is managed and financed. This may include sole proprietorship, partnership, or corporation. It's important to choose the right structure based on personal goals, liability protection, and tax considerations. Consulting with legal and financial professionals can help make this decision.

Payroll

Payroll refers to the total amount of money paid by a salon to its employees for their work. Careful management of payroll is essential for the financial success of a hair salon. Before starting a salon, it is important to analyze potential payroll costs to ensure that they are sustainable for the business.

Perming

Perming is the process of chemically altering the hair to create a permanent wave or curl. This service can be offered at a hair salon and requires specialized training and equipment. Before investing in a hair salon, it is important to ensure that the staff is well-trained in performing perms to ensure customer satisfaction and safety.

Personal protective equipment

Personal protective equipment (PPE) refers to gear worn by salon employees to protect them from exposure to harsh chemicals and other hazards. It is important for a salon to invest in high-quality PPE for its employees to ensure their health and safety while on the job.

Point-of-sale system

A point-of-sale (POS) system is a computerized system used to manage sales transactions, inventory, and customer data. A hair salon requires a reliable POS system to manage customer transactions and track inventory. It is important to invest in a high-quality POS system that can handle the unique needs of a hair salon.

Pricing strategy

A pricing strategy is a plan for setting the prices of goods or services offered by a business. Before starting or investing in a hair salon, it is important to develop a pricing strategy that takes into account factors such as competition, location, and target clientele.

Product inventory

Product inventory refers to the stock of hair care products that a salon offers for sale to its customers. It is important for a salon to carefully manage its product inventory, ensuring that it is well-stocked with in-demand products while avoiding overstocking and wasting money. A successful hair salon invests in high-quality products and frequently updates its inventory to meet the changing needs of its customers.

Professional development

Professional development refers to the ongoing education and training that salon staff undergo to improve their skills and stay up-to-date with industry trends. A successful hair salon invests in the professional development of its staff to ensure that they offer the best possible service to their customers.

Professional liability insurance

Professional liability insurance provides financial protection to a business in the event that a customer sues the business due to negligence or a mistake made by its employees. A hair salon should invest in professional liability insurance to ensure that it is protected from potential legal and financial consequences.

Profit margin

Profit margin represents the percentage of revenue that a business retains after deducting its expenses. Before starting or investing in a hair salon, it is important to carefully analyze and project potential revenue and expenses to determine a profitable pricing structure that will result in a healthy profit margin.

Promotion

Promotion refers to the marketing and advertising efforts made by a salon to attract customers and increase sales. Before starting a salon, it is important to develop a strong promotion strategy that effectively communicates the salon's brand and services to potential customers.

Recurring revenue

Income generated by ongoing services or products offered to clients on a regular basis, such as monthly subscription services or product refills. Recurring revenue can contribute to the salon's stability and profitability if managed effectively.

Referrals

Word-of-mouth recommendations from satisfied customers that lead to new clients. Encouraging referrals through promotions, incentives, or excellent service can significantly boost the salon's customer base and revenue. Providing incentives to existing customers for referring new clients is an effective strategy for increasing referrals.

Regulations

Laws and rules that govern the establishment and operation of a hair salon. Such regulations include licensing requirements, building codes, sanitation standards, zoning laws, and labor laws. Failing to comply with regulations can lead to fines or even the closure of the salon.

Renovation

The process of updating or improving the salon's physical space, furniture, equipment, or decor. Renovations can make the salon more attractive to customers, improve functionality, and enhance the overall look and feel of the space. However, renovations can also be costly and disruptive to business, so careful planning and budgeting are essential.

Rent

The amount of money paid to the landlord or property owner for the use of salon space. Before investing in or starting a hair salon, it is essential to determine whether the rent is reasonable and negotiate the terms of the lease agreement, including rent increases, lease renewals, and the length of the lease.

Reputation

The public perception of the hair salon based on its quality of service, customer satisfaction, and overall performance in the market over time. Maintaining a good reputation requires delivering excellent service, advertising, and marketing, maintaining a clean and professional facility, and effectively resolving customer complaints.

Retail

The sale of hair care products, accessories, and other merchandise in the salon. Retail sales can be a significant source of revenue for a hair salon, and selecting the right products and effectively marketing them can boost profits.

Returns

The percentage of customers who return to the salon for repeat services. High return rates indicate customer satisfaction and loyalty, which are critical to the salon's success. Maintaining a high level of service quality and offering promotions and rewards to regular customers can increase return rates.

Revenue

The total income generated by the hair salon from all sources, such as hair styling services, product sales, and rental fees. Monitoring revenue is key to managing the salon's finances and ensuring profitability. Revenue can be maximized through good marketing and cost controls.

Rich media

The use of images, videos, and interactive content on the hair salon's website and social media profiles to showcase services, staff, and promotions. Rich media can help attract and retain clients, increase brand awareness, and improve search engine rankings.

Salon Decor

The decor of a salon can affect the mood and atmosphere of the salon, and therefore clients' experience. Choose a decor style that reflects the brand and attracts a target demographic.

Salon Location

Finding the right location for the salon is crucial for success. Consider factors such as accessibility, visibility, and competition when choosing the location.

Salon Management Software

This is a computer program that can help salon owners manage their salon better. It can help with scheduling appointments, managing employees, tracking inventory and sales, and tracking customer information. This software can improve efficiency and save time and money.

Salon Suite

A self-contained space in a salon where an individual stylist can work with their clients privately. This is a great option for stylists who are just starting out and want to build their clientele in a more personalized space.

Sanitation and Sterilization

Proper sanitation and sterilization practices in a salon are important for the health and safety of clients and staff. The salon should have a system in place to maintain cleanliness and prevent the spread of infection.

Service Menu

A list of services offered in a salon with their corresponding prices. It is important to have a detailed and specific service menu to avoid confusion and misunderstandings with clients.

Social Media Marketing

Maintaining an online presence through social media platforms such as Facebook, Twitter, and Instagram can help to promote the salon and attract new clients.

Staff Management

Managing employees in a hair salon is crucial for success. It includes things like scheduling, training, supervision, setting goals and providing feedback. Happy employees will create a happy work environment for everyone.

Stylist Commission

How much a stylist earns is an important factor to consider before starting or investing in a salon. Most salons pay their stylists a commission based off of the services they provide.

Target Market

The group or demographic of customers that the hair salon intends to cater to. It is important to understand the target market, including its age range, income, needs, and preferences, to be able to create relevant and effective marketing strategies, services, and products.

Taxation

Understanding tax laws and regulations related to operating a hair salon is essential. It includes taxation on the business, employees, and products and services offered. This involves hiring a knowledgeable accountant or financial advisor to provide guidance on taxes, financial planning, and compliance.

Techniques

Different hair techniques, such as cutting, coloring, and styling, require specialized skills and knowledge. It is important to remain up-to-date with industry standards and techniques to provide high-quality services and remain competitive in the market.

Tenancy Agreements

A tenancy agreement is a legally binding contract between the landlord and tenant that outlines the terms and conditions of renting a space for a hair salon. It includes details on rent, duration, maintenance, and any other relevant obligations and rights. It is important to obtain a clear and fair tenancy agreement to avoid any future disputes or issues.

Termination

Effective termination policies and procedures should be established when hiring employees to protect the business and ensure fair treatment. This includes creating clear employment contracts, expectations, and disciplinary procedures, as well as documenting and addressing any issues or violations.

Time Management

Proper time management is essential for a hair salon to operate smoothly and efficiently. It includes scheduling appointments, managing staff schedules, and prioritizing tasks to meet deadlines and customer expectations. It also involves effectively managing any unforeseen events or emergencies that arise.

Tools and Equipment

Hair salons require a range of tools and equipment, such as scissors, combs, hair dryers, and chairs, to perform services effectively. It is important to invest in high-quality tools and equipment to ensure durability and efficiency, as well as regular maintenance to extend their lifespan.

Training

Proper training is crucial for the success of a hair salon. This includes attending cosmetology school, apprenticeships, continuing education courses, and certification programs to stay up-to-date with the latest trends, techniques, and regulations in the industry. Training also encompasses the hiring and management of skilled and reliable staff members to ensure consistent quality service.

Treatments

Hair salons offer a variety of treatment options, such as deep conditioning, scalp treatments, and extensions. Understanding the benefits and risks of each treatment, as well as their cost and demand, is crucial to provide high-quality services and generate revenue. It also involves selecting the appropriate products and tools to use for each treatment.

Trends

Keeping up with current hair trends is critical for attracting and retaining customers. It involves researching and implementing new hair styles, products, and techniques, as well as staying knowledgeable about the latest fashion and beauty trends.

Understanding Salon Software

Salon software can be used to manage appointments, track inventory, and manage financials for a hair salon. It's important to understand how to use and customize salon software to ensure it meets the specific needs of the business and improves efficiency.

Understanding Your Target Market

A crucial step in starting or investing in a hair salon is understanding the demographics of the target market. This includes factors such as age, gender, income level, and geographic location. Understanding the target market can inform decisions on location, pricing, services offered, and marketing strategies.

Unforeseen Expenses

Unexpected expenses can arise when starting or investing in a hair salon, such as unexpected repairs or upgrades, licensing fees, or legal costs. It's important to have a contingency plan and reserve funds for unforeseen expenses to avoid financial strain on the business.

Uniforms

Clothing worn by employees of a hair salon that is consistent and promotes a professional appearance. Uniforms can also help customers easily identify employees and promote the brand image of the salon. They can range from simple logo shirts to more elaborate outfits depending on the salon's style and budget.

Unique Selling Proposition

A unique selling proposition (USP) is what sets a hair salon apart from its competitors and makes it stand out to potential customers. This might be a particular service or product, a unique salon atmosphere or decor, or exceptional customer service.

Upkeep

Maintenance and upkeep of the salon space and equipment is important to ensure a safe and comfortable environment for clients and employees. This includes regular cleaning, equipment repairs, and replacing any worn or outdated items in the salon.

Upselling

The practice of encouraging clients to purchase additional services or products beyond what they originally planned on. Upselling can increase revenue and profits for a hair salon, but should be done in a subtle and respectful manner to avoid making customers feel pressured or uncomfortable.

Upskilling

Regular training and upskilling for employees can improve the quality of services offered by a hair salon and enhance customer satisfaction. This might include training in advanced techniques, product knowledge, or customer service skills.

User Experience

The user experience (UX) is how clients perceive and interact with the salon from the moment they walk in the door. This includes factors such as ease of making appointments, comfort and cleanliness of the salon environment, and quality of customer service. A positive user experience is essential to building a loyal customer base and driving repeat business.

Utilities

Essential services such as water, electricity, and gas that are needed to operate a hair salon. It's important to understand the costs associated with these utilities and factor them into the salon's budget and business plan.

Value Chain Analysis

A process of evaluating the various stages of the salon's operations, from acquiring products to delivering services to customers, to identify areas in which the salon can increase efficiency and profitability.

Value Proposition

The unique selling point of a hair salon that sets it apart from competitors. This includes the salon's level of service, quality of products used, and pricing strategy.

Variable Costs

Expenses that vary based on the level of production or services provided by the salon. This includes costs such as wages for stylists and cost of supplies.

Vendor Management

The process of identifying and managing suppliers of products, equipment, and services needed to run a hair salon. This includes negotiating prices, managing relationships, and ensuring timely delivery.

Venture Capital

A type of investment funding for startups or small businesses, which can provide capital for a hair salon in exchange for equity or ownership shares.

Venue Selection

The process of choosing the physical location for the hair salon. Factors to consider include foot traffic, accessibility, and competition in the area.

Virtual Bookkeeping

Using digital tools and software to manage the financial records and transactions of the hair salon. This includes tracking revenue and expenses, managing payroll, and preparing financial statements.

Virtual Marketing

Using digital marketing methods and social media platforms to promote and advertise the hair salon to potential customers. This includes strategies such as paid advertising, influencer partnerships, and email marketing.

Vision Statement

A statement outlining the long-term goals and aspirations of the hair salon. This can include information on the salon's target market, service offerings, and growth plans.

Volume Rebates

Discounts or rebates offered by suppliers or manufacturers based on the volume of products or equipment purchased by the hair salon.

Wages

Refers to the salary or hourly wage paid to employees by a hair salon. Employees are the backbone of any business; hence, it is crucial to pay them adequately. The wages should be competitive enough to attract and retain skilled workers. It helps to ensure high-quality service provision.

Walk-ins

Refers to customers who do not have an appointment and show up at the hair salon seeking services. Accommodating walk-ins improves customer satisfaction, but it is essential to balance walk-ins with scheduled appointments to avoid confusion and delays.

Waste management

Refers to activities and procedures implemented to reduce and dispose of waste generated in the hair salon. Hair salons produce substantial waste, such as chemical residue, hair clippings, and single-use products. Proper waste management reduces environmental impact and ensures compliance with regulations.

Water conservation

Measures put in place to reduce the use of water in the hair salon. Water is a precious resource that should be used responsibly. Implementing water conservation practices, such as using low-flow faucets, reusing towels, and upgrading to water-efficient equipment, can save money and reduce environmental impact.

Website development

Creating an online platform to market and promote the hair salon's services. A well-designed website with relevant and up-to-date information can attract and retain clients. The website should be user-friendly, mobile-responsive, and optimized for search engines.

Wholesale buying

Purchasing salon supplies like shampoo, conditioners, hair color, and hair care products directly from a manufacturer or a distributor at a discounted rate. Buying in bulk reduces the cost of products, which can be advantageous to a hair salon business. A wise purchasing strategy can help to increase profit margin.

Work environment

The overall atmosphere, culture, and conditions of the hair salon. A good work environment enhances productivity, teamwork, and employee morale. Factors that contribute to a positive work environment include equipment, lighting, cleanliness, safety, and employee benefits.

Worker's compensation

Insurance that provides benefits to employees who suffer injuries or illnesses while on the job. Hair salon workers are prone to cuts, burns, and other injuries, making worker's compensation a crucial consideration.

Workflow

The series of steps that a customer undergoes while getting a service in a hair salon. It starts from booking an appointment, consultation, service provision to payment. It is essential to establish a well-organized and efficient workflow to provide high-quality and timely services to customers.

Workforce management

The hiring, training, scheduling, and monitoring of hair salon employees to ensure efficient operations. Managing the workforce involves delegating duties, supervising employees' performance, and addressing staffing issues. Ensuring the workforce aligns with the hair salon's goals can increase productivity and boost customer satisfaction.